CAPE POETRY PAPERBACKS

JENI COUZYN
MONKEYS' WEDDING

by the same author

FLYING

TWELVE TO TWELVE (*editor*)

Jeni Couzyn

MONKEYS' WEDDING

JONATHAN CAPE
THIRTY BEDFORD SQUARE LONDON

FIRST PUBLISHED 1972
THIS PAPERBACK EDITION FIRST PUBLISHED 1973
© 1972 BY JENI COUZYN

JONATHAN CAPE LTD
30 BEDFORD SQUARE LONDON WC1

ISBN 0 224 00825 0

Condition of Sale

This book is sold subject to the condition that it shall not, by way of trade or otherwise, be lent, re-sold, hired out, or otherwise circulated without the publisher's prior consent, in any form of binding or cover other than that in which it is published and without a similar condition including this condition being imposed on the subsequent purchaser.

Thanks are due to Radios 1, 2 and 3, where some of these poems were first broadcast, and to *Workshop* magazine, where others first appeared. Also to the Globe Playhouse Trust, who commissioned 'Song Of The Drinker Of Juices' for their 1972 Shakespeare birthday celebration, and to the Runnymede Trust, who commissioned 'Song Of The Women Of Islington' for the film *It's Ours Whatever They Say*.
'There Are Some Creatures Living In My Body' was first published in *Pollute and Be Damned* by Arthur Bourne (Dent, 1972).

*Printed and bound in Great Britain
by Richard Clay (The Chaucer Press) Ltd, Bungay, Suffolk*

Contents

A Plan For Parting
The Heir 14
The Way Towards Each Other Is Through Our Bodies 16
The Wife 17
The Babies 18
Vision 19
Morning 20
My Best Mona Lisa 21
The Poet 22
A Warning To Blood Suckers 24
I Should Have Done With These Fancy Gentlemen 25
Poem For An Abandoned Species 26
Love 4 27
Tom's Widow At The Christmas Party 28
Mr Hieronymus Oxford 29
Mr Hieronymus Oxford Hears The Dawn Chorus 30
You Have To Say You Like It 32
Miss Jane Bird's Last Armageddon 34
Miss Jane Bird Resists Temptation 36
Miss Jane Bird Takes A Long Look At Reality 39
Miss Jane Bird Discovers That She Is A Prophet 40
Go, go. 41

Notes To The Designer
Specimen 2001, Probably 21c 44
A Zoo Sequence 46
Cassandra In Tears On Putney Common 50
Houdini Foresees His Death 53
Specimen 69 54
Song 55
Don't Worry They'll Find A Bed For You Too 56
The King Of The Cats Is Dead 58
Song Of The Women Of Islington 60
There Are Some Creatures Living In My Body 61

The Return

The Return   64
The Reunion   65
The Shepherd   66
The Interrogation   67
Poor Little Bird   68
The House Of Jealousy   69
The Beast   70
The Trial   72
The Door   74
Poem For Alice   75
We Found Him Amid Stones   76
Ndumu   78
Elephant Song   79

Songs

Song Of The Drinker of Juices   82
Song Of The Almost Remembered   84
Giving Song   86
Song Of The Flying Baboon   88
Hymn For A Stranger   90
Complaint Of The Water   92
Song Of The Taken Care Of   93

**for Jafar
keeper of door
and skylight**

'Nyugmo nne,
Hunu ntso,
Ogboole nfo
   enibiiahe'

A Plan For Parting

The Heir

How we prepared for you. Nights
carefully, we would climb
into the long darkness
where you were lurking
made for you new
arms and head and
small new body to begin again in.
Nights out of our love for each other
we made you that small body.
We created it, meticulous, patiently.
How we were God making it.
It was perfect. A house. A safe
house to be at ease in.

Clasped on the verge
of the desert where you walk
how we called out your name
that we were ready.
We called out your name
where you were withered and poison
in the shredded dark.

From the edge, the brink
you watch us without eyes.
The softness of bodies the warm
house we have prepared for you.
You would leap across the darkness
but you have no body.
You would weep
but you have no voice.
You would cry out to us to
come
and find you, but we can't hear.

You watch us call you without eyes.
O here there is no way in.
Here is all flesh and hard bone.
Child.
They are pouring bandages on your
broken house.

The Way Towards Each Other Is Through Our Bodies

The way towards each other is through our bodies.
Words are the longest distance you can travel
so complex and hazardous you
lose your direction.

Time is no way either. A river mouth it opens
to a mixing of waters, a tidal
diffusion, never
a consummation.

In our bodies we are fallen in a thorn thicket.
Out is a tearing apart, a letting of juices.
Inside though is a pathway, a tremulous compensation —
the possibility of touching.

The Wife

if you entered

where there were strange smelling rare foods laid out
in vine leaves
you might first find her. she wouldn't notice you staring
her eyes at ease.

her flesh delicately wrapped
on fine bones. her hair the cared for kind.
her nails smooth and clean. her clothes that fresh
cloth that only wives wear

with small flowers on it. soft skirts
lap on pale calves. she fingers the food
wisely. the attendant in his white coat politely
breathes.

if she raised her eyes she would make him
wither. she has centuries of her kind
flicking their eyes
behind her. she could make anyone feel slight.

nightly she glides through girls dreams, they always
avoiding her eye.
touching her arm is the stranger
whose face is hidden. together their curved backs

would move away into light.

The Babies

When I returned, my husband
was drying his hands on a towel.

I'm afraid I've made
a bit of a mess, he said.

On the table the baby lay
pulped like a water melon, a few

soft bits of skull protruding from the mush.
She hardly cried at all he said.

The rock, sticky with flesh on its
sharp edges, lay beside the body.

Well, that's that, said my beloved.
I smoothed a little of the stuff

from his upper arm that he had missed
when performing his ablutions.

I suppose you wonder why I wrote this poem.
I expect you'll say its nasty, *gratuitously*

nasty, summing the matter up.

Suppose I say I have written it
for women. For modern, reasonable women

lying silent between sheets
that stink of decaying semen.

Vision

On the first day he struck
love into her vein. Suddenly she uncurled
like mint long without rain.

On the second day she told the old
gatherer to go away.
A gang of leaves was waiting at the door.

On the third day he showed her
the inside of his head. She gathered the ragged
pieces together.

On the fourth day they caught sight of
Sir Chubley Knight in the light-metered
sun, remote,

squirrel drinking at his throat
smoking a cigar in his double-breasted
waistcoat:

That was the day the world
sprang from its perfect hiding place shouting
Here I am! Here I am!

Morning

You are too naked for touching.
If I stroke your brown skin
as you sleep you may break. I irritate
your long dreams. I depress your awakening. I am
no good for you in your alien habitation.

Waiting for you to wake I wait
for a return from a long voyage, not knowing
what scurvy violence you bring back
to embarrass my clean house. Wherever I sow
perfection it grows into weeds. O my beautiful

How time changes the clean seed, how the corruption
of absence on my body, my damp hands. Awake
I am in sleep also, treacherous and lonely.
I don't know where to go, where to find rest.
Come back.

My Best Mona Lisa

I would like to see that girl's smile
disappearing in a liquidizer along with the
leeks and turnips.

The Poet

Behind glass
he sees the bullet
tear into flesh
sees the girl scream.
He watches from his
chaise-longue
his calm wife beside him.
She has cooked a plain
meal
(his stomach isn't strong)
and now he feels
content.

    Behind glass the girl
    writhes. People in white coats
    gather about her.
    Twitching she breaks
    free of their good arms.
    She hurls herself
    against the glass. He sees her
    cry out, clawing,
    blood under her nails.
    He notes
    each detail.

Holding a microphone
close to his lips
he reasons with her
explains
that his wife is beginning to fear
for the safety of
the screen.
Her lips
move like a fish.

One of the people in
white coats
has noticed him
begins to walk across the room
towards him.
Hastily he draws
velvet across the screen.
He puts away his gun.
It is time for coffee in
small cups.

A Warning To Blood Suckers

This is my pain.
I rejoice in its
possession.

No-one shares it, no doctors wisely
confer to
disguise it, no men

tangle their arms and pulpy
lips about me to
shield me from it:

this is my pain. I drink it
clean and lethal in my vein.

No one come near me.

I Should Have Done With These Fancy Gentlemen

I should have done with these
fancy gentlemen
should find me someone
tender and young without a pantry full of
dead women.
Should find me a pretty boy
naked in sun baiting lobsters
for a living
one
who never heard of poetry
killed his mother and
doesn't feel guilty,
flings rocks at beggars to
test his catapult, sets his dogs on visitors
for fresh meat,
swims lazy among sharks in the early morning
spear quivering
cup of pearls between his teeth.

Poem For An Abandoned Species

Don't worry
it isn't like they said
hands clawing darkness
convulsion, blood
oozing from the nostril
the horror.

It is nestled in warm feathers
soft in straw
white, fragile.

When day comes
With her packing cases and
sharp knife

you are deeply
asleep.
Don't wriggle anymore.

Love 4

You are vanished.
I thought we were still very young.
Tonight in this bed
one
peeled
body
hugging itself.
Tonight in the street white new snow
would click under our feet.

Tom's Widow At The Christmas Party

I'll turn the cards up to make them
good for you
that's the jewellery you wear
the three diamonds
a black haired woman and a black haired man
turned their backs on one another

That club man is jacking thoughts
on a girl in a garden

You'll face
deep water in a tomb
there's a woman has good hearts for you
a marriage settlement and a surprise
a short journey a kiss
in a bright house
There's good hearts to your wish
and there's jealousy

A black haired woman and a black haired man
turned their backs on one another

That club man is jacking thoughts
on a girl in a garden.

Mr Hieronymus Oxford

is a reasonable man.
For him loving is an intellectual
hobby
that he knows he's no good at.
He doesn't hold with emotions.
He lives in a polythene bag
and sometimes masturbates to
make himself quiver
or remembers the way he murdered
his mother and father to
make himself cry.

He is a cold fish gliding around my life
with flat eyes
snapping up morsels of distress
that float from my shredded self like
excrement into water.

One day as I beat my head on the floor
weeping, he suddenly said
'Is loving your career?'
He'd had a vision of something
resembling reality
and it appalled him.

If he is water
he lies quite still in a muddy
pool so as not to disturb himself.
You'll never get a glimpse of
sky on his face
or hear rumour of oceans.

Mr Hieronymus Oxford Hears The Dawn Chorus

I watch you
absurd in the half-light
clambering into soiled clothes.

Your mutterings of love
hang, funny faces in the air
sniggering.

Your haste is pornographic,
comical.
You blunder about feeling clumsy

like a huge hairy baboon
shattering the pale trees.
You are thinking of your knobbly knees.

I watch you
serene from my white sheets.
Soon I shall be abandoned

naked and in tears on a ruined
love-bed.
You in black leather restored

will whiz down the Richmond road
in your sportscar, touching eighty
feeling a man

but not quite yet. First this, our
laughter—listen
there is no avoiding it

and the room bristling with eyes
bright, watchful
glistening with malice

mine, your wife's, and all your lost
mistresses
before the tears come.

You Have To Say You Like It

The room smelt of
sickness. Curtains
had covered the windows for days. No light had
entered and shadows clung
dead things in corners.
The room smelt of decay and fever.

On the bed she lay
wrapped in a cocoon of wool and old
skin. Her body had a grey
unused look. Her eyelids were rimmed
wide open from constant pain. Her face
dented as though someone had been kicking at it with
padded boots looked dimly
surprised.

Her body was curled
into itself to cover shame from
enraged mobs that would
storm in on her. The walls were too thin and
no locks would hold the doors. Windows were
thin glass. They were swarming in where she lay
exposed like a broken egg in a stale
pool of herself. They poured
howling down the telephone. The doorbell
was ringing and ringing.
The windows were lined with ready knuckles of
sharp bone. The bedcovers
wouldn't hold.
She gripped them tightly over her eyes.

Someone slipped in and said he would
drive away the faces. He took a great stick and
turned upon her, eyes glinting.
Where she lay peering from a
puffed face hair in strands salt from weeping he
kissed the soles of her two feet. Then he
went out of the door. The world was howling at her to
rise, and say she liked it, and make a
contribution.

Miss Jane Bird's Last Armageddon

I shall start off buying hundreds and
hundreds of
pretty panties in
neat rows smelling
sweetly of lavender
and hang my dresses in order

Then
new sheets for my three quarter
bed which is neither
double nor single
bright
red with pillows to match

Every morning a
soft boiled egg for breakfast
with wholewheat
bread and real butter
sitting at a table

Face masks and
manicures pampering my body I shall
bathe in perfumes

Participate in
humanity start
answering letters
cheating on the underground
buying
newspapers
to read about
the wars

Now that at last nothing
spectacular and
lovely has
befallen me
I can't hang on any longer
I'm going to
accept this absurd ridiculous inhospitable
Jane Bird
for a house.

Miss Jane Bird Resists Temptation

Met this man
had a gang of women
tearing each other into red
bloody bits in a cage.
Some were ghosts but so real
you couldn't tell the live
from the dead.
—'Ere, 'e says to me
want to come in?
—No thanks mate
I've been in one of those.
—But this is art he says
—No thanks I said
I know about art and that
I've decided on
happiness.
—Happiness he says
You must be joking.
Art, he says, A.R.T. Poetry.
—I know I said
That poem you got in your
head now though
has five dead women an
a couple of kids—
stiffs
in it. I've decided on survival.
Then this poet fellow gets real mad.
—Look. he says.
They adore me.
They all adore me.
Nobody ever resisted me. I'm
adorable.
Everyone says so.

The women in the cage
screamed and snarled
stretching their bloody arms
out at us through the bars.
—Look at that. he says.
They adore me. You *bitch* you'll
destroy my confidence.
Tough mate I said
I'm not going in. No.
(I'm acting smooth and easy now
like I thought the world was soft snow)
—Look he says.
he gets down on his knees
he's trembling all over
I can see he's nearly crying
an his fly's undone
He's got underpants sky blue
—Look.
the world needs me.
Think of how many kids an that
died in wars
not loving nobody
an nothing to show for it
nothing.
He picks up some books of words
an shoves them at me
turning the pages quick
an touching them all over with his palm
—Look at em all just you LOOK
he says
I never wasted nothing
There ain't been a cry in my life
not recorded and wrote down
not one, he says.

You want to take away my living?
my meat?
the blood out of my very mouth?
—Yes I said
the more poets an that unplugged
the better
far as I can see.
An I walked away
leaving him there on the gravel
his women in the cage
raise a great wail and begin
tearing each other again but
I walks out of there I don't know
where, over the hills.

Miss Jane Bird Takes A Long Look At Reality

You lose on the roundabout
what you gain on the swings but
there's little comfort in the law of
averages
sighed miss Jane Bird, trailing
oiled wings.

Miss Jane Bird Discovers That She Is A Prophet

One day miss jane bird
heard her heart beat.
Here I am—here I am
she thought, half-way between
birth and the death-sack
and I haven't begun yet.
I think in whispers from
inside a box,
the world has to be filtered
to a fine silt for my palate,
I'm afraid most of the time—
the rest I'm asleep.

The world, said miss jane bird
is nothing really to be afraid of.
Life should be squandered
lightly.
I waste all my time
preparing myself. The others—the
unkind—they haven't really damaged me.
Here I am between my skull and my
toes
in tact, said jane bird, spinster, of
timid disposition.

Miss Jane Bird collected her used
years, packed them neatly into a sainsbury's
carrier bag, gave away
the hopes she'd been saving
to the lady upstairs
and went to live in Lapland.

Go, go.

miniature
looped in gold
a temple

the cage.

Wide where the door was
dead the bird
nail through its wing.

Notes To The Designer

Specimen 2001, Probably 21c
(on an ancient manuscript)

Dear Aunty May,

Last week after the news I sent off some
express letters.
I sent them to

The Human Inhabitant, The White House, USA,
The Human Inhabitant, The Kremlin, USSR and
The Human Inhabitant, 10 Downing Street, UK.

Inside the letters I wrote: You must not send
people to the wars because they have told me
they don't want to kill a species they

haven't seen.
                The Post Office
returned the letters to me unopened.
On the envelope they wrote: Address Unknown.

So then I sent express letters to all the Human
Inhabitants, in all the houses in the world.
Inside the letters I wrote:

STOP PRESS: If you don't want to go to the wars
(like you keep telling me) then you needn't.
There are no longer Human Inhabitants

governing the world.
                The Post Office
returned all those letters to me as well:
Address Unknown.

That's how I discovered it.
The Post Office wouldn't lie.
There aren't any Human Inhabitants in the world.

There are a lot of explosions around the stars.
I feel lonely.

In case of miracles like you used to believe in
I am going to put this letter into a bottle
and throw it into the sea. Love from Eve.

A Zoo Sequence

Yellow Baboon

The yellow baboon
his organ a pink dying stalk
masturbates, legs spread wide
without interest—as one would casually
peel a banana
looking around him.
When his moment of
passion comes, I detect a faint
irritation
as he hooks the toes of his two feet together
and straightens his knees.
Then he lifts the white fruit from the limp
stalk, and eats it
rudely, without enjoyment, dipping his finger
carefully to scoop the last drops.

Squirrel

See the way a caged squirrel
at feeding time
will tear the nut open
his small face trembling over the
stainless steel dish.

Sea-Eagle

—Why are his wings so big?
 Why?
Because they are.
—But why?
Because he is heavy
he has to go
up in the air.
—Why does he sit
 with his wings
 stretched out like that
 filling his cage?

Wolf

Savage things asleep
look gentle
and is this softly breathing the
enemy, who stole your sheep?

Rhinoceros

Inside that lump of granite
blood flows
cells break
somewhere you are.
Behind that small black hole
images float again
somewhere in there I am
somewhere, where you are.

The Small Insect House

All these small creatures
attend to themselves
the millipede very slowly
sucks tiny parasite flecks from
his long black shell
combing it carefully with his
million fine legs—
Stick insect
hermit crab
praying mantis that was
sacred to bushmen.

               Lemur

               Lemur fingers glass with
               small paws
               where frosted light
               falls gently.

The Slow Lorris

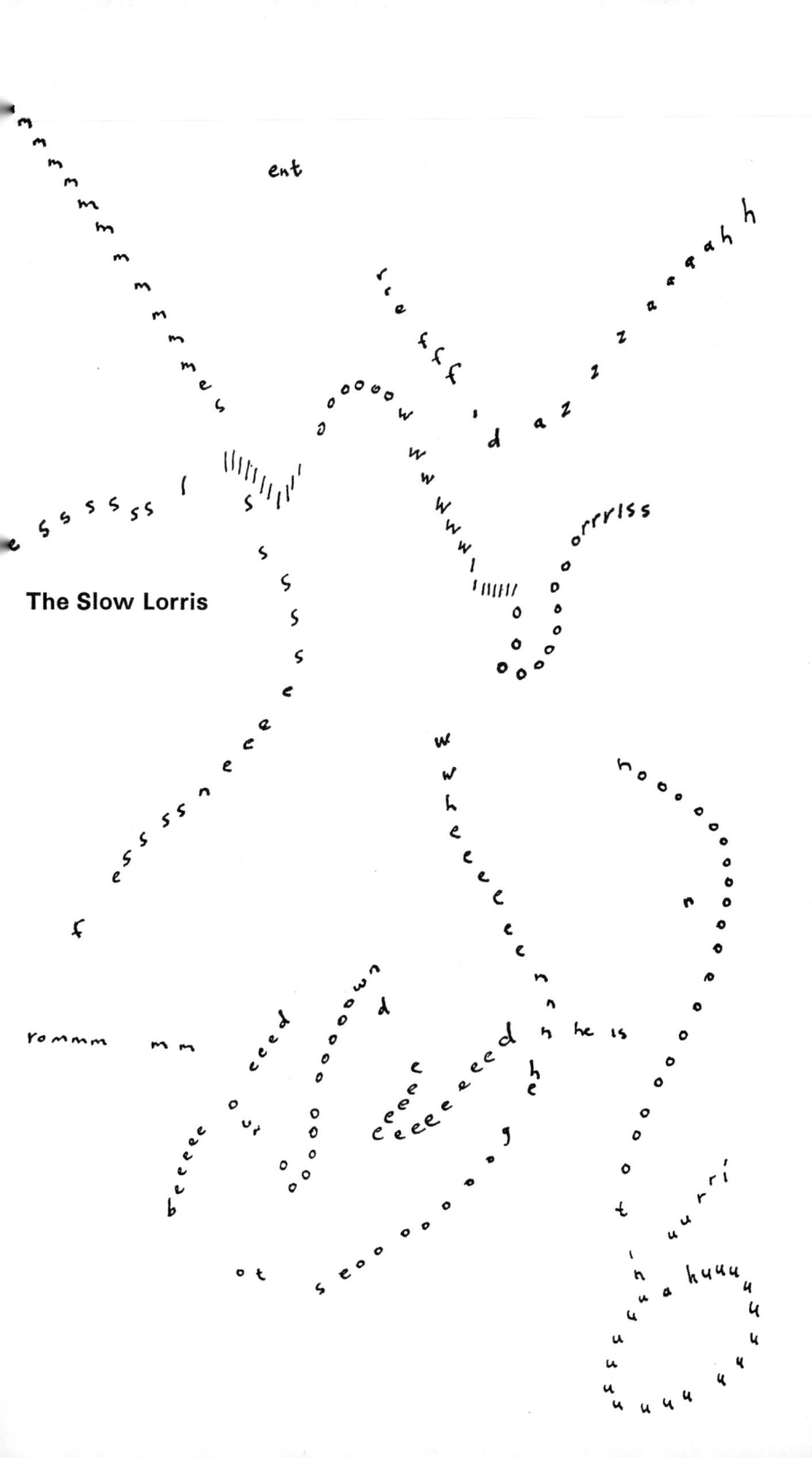

Cassandra In Tears On Putney Common

'We are all going to go zoom
off together on a big mushroom

we knew it was going to happen.
We knew we were going to
make it happen
but we were so busy killing each other
in Vietnam, and Lebanon and
wherever we could get a bit of
pain in
that we didn't have much time
for worrying.

In some parts of the universe now
they call it pride
how the human species committed
suicide out of
nausea for itself.
Somewhere else they say
bravely humanity died to fulfil
a prophecy it found in a book.

It might look
easy like that to them but
none of us
wanted it to happen.
No-one I know wants it to happen.
No-one my friends know
wants it to happen.

It's hard to believe though.
In London alone we lived
happily for years making more and more
money till we had enough bombs
to destroy the earth
four times over.

I also. But I didn't feel as if I did it
more than birds or whales.
I thought I was screaming
for them to make it stop.
Everybody on earth distinctly heard himself
screaming to each other to make it
stop.
We were all screaming when we did it.
We were all screaming STOP.
There was a lot of noise.

Not from the animals.
They crumpled suddenly from their nests
not understanding
and insects flared bright their wings.
We didn't mean it to happen.
We didn't like the earth all
ended and fused in glass.
We didn't like our bodies hiss
and blacken our eyeballs melt
WE DON'T LIKE PAIN we didn't
want it to happen.
Nobody I knew wanted it to happen.
We were a species fond of trees
and things that moved.

Right till the end
people were still praying for
death by water or
a brick across the skull.

It was over so soon.
And it didn't help being afraid
of THE THING once we'd made it.
Bombs are stronger than you are
and understand their function.

BOOOOOOOOOOOOOOMMMMMMMMMMMM'

Houdini Foresees His Death
(a slow chant)

hòun houdòunin hounàdou
dòun dòuah hounànin
dounàdinah hòuah noudàhoun
dòuah hounànoun hòuah

dìn dìah dinàdah
nadànin nìn nadàninah
nìdah nìdahou nìdahah
hàan hànin hadàninah

hòudahah hìd hòudahah
nìdahin nìdah nadàninah
hànin hànin hòudahah
dòun dòuah dounàhah

Specimen 69

This small soft male was found in a whitish pack in the northern area.

It was being cared for by the tribe who also regarded it with revulsion.

The species gives tender support to those members it mentally despises

killing those it favours, often in large numbers.

This curious specimen is the first so far discovered with

a handle in its back. DO NOT FEED.

Song

Fool, how would you destroy the world?
With green jelly master. All things
flowing I would stop up.
Clot jelly in vein and stem
creep on things moving, and seal them
green slime everywhere cling and
quivering. Thus. Thus I would seal up the world
in green translucence.

Fool, and how would you save it?
Whiteness. Whiteness master.
I would drain all colour from fish and mountain
sleeve of silk and butterfly
fairground and daisy chain and
forest and artifact. White. All white.
Thus I would save the world
by opening, opening my master.

Don't Worry They'll Find A Bed For You Too

One day I looked out of the window and saw
the hospital
the brand new big hospital that would cure all known
diseases
A triumph of Medical Science over Bacteria
said the sign
There will be no more Suffering
All pain henceforth is Computer Controlled.

But have you eliminated death
I asked a man without a face in a white overall.
No he said. We can't afford to eliminate death.
Not with the birth-rate you lot keep going.
The way you lot breed
he said. Like bacteria. He spat.
I secretly thanked my good luck that my body had so far
held up strong.

I didn't like the idea of his kind
taking me over.
But the next day I looked out of the window and saw
that the hospital had grown.
Three blocks up the street and the cranes
like a net over the sky
concrete and girders and everywhere people in white overalls
hurrying.

What about all the noise you are making
I asked one of the faceless ones.
O the machines make a bit of noise, he said
have to when they're working
but think of how great it will be when it's finished
he said
ploughing up the last few willow trees
and the tom thumb nursery school.

The next day the whole of Hampstead was part of
her majesty's royal free hospital.
I fled to Kentish Town but the hospital
followed after.
Huge bulldozers marked PROGRESS ripped up houses
I was almost bricked into ward 2,000 by accident
when I fell asleep in the barrel I was hiding in.
It was time to get out:

I went to live in the country.
On my first morning I woke thinking of cows and wild
oxalis. I opened the little old wooden front door
and stretched. Then I opened my eyes and saw
the hospital, striding over the hills towards me
like a malignant giant. Its no good
it said. I'll get you in the end. But I am alright
I said. I don't have any ulcers, tumours, blood clots

varicose veins, broken bones, neuroses or psychoses.
You will, it said, you will. Soon I shall cover the whole
world, but don't worry. The computers will find
a bed for you somewhere. There are plenty of wards
for everyone. All will be provided with
a comfortable bacteria free scientifically controlled
place to die in. Don't you worry about a thing.
I *am* worried, I said, *I am bloody, sickeningly worried.*

Ha Ha it said.

The King Of The Cats Is Dead

The king of the cats is dead
Tom the all time conqueror
Tom the invincible bushytailed
Tom the monarch of eternity.
Hazel-eyed
he could see around the world
knew the hiding places of birds
terror of rats and squirrels he
played games on the wild heath
with credible pretty witches
Tom the slant-eyed
Tom the cunning deceitful trickster of men
Tom the hero among cats
Tom the wise of many generations.

Alas Tom is dead.
I sing his praises who would not have noticed
contemptible me. Alas Tom the hero
I see you everywhere, in black cats
everywhere I am looking for you
who betrayed you.
Your yellow eyes plague my vision.

The king of the cats is dead.
They are building the Royal Free
where he ruled generations of cats who were
knights among cats, the round table of
noble cats, the merry men among cats
scorning the dandy domestics.
Wildcat of dustbin and midnight
they were sovereign
where whitecoated men lurk now in the
old places, scum of the earth with your nets and
poised syringes, a pox on your endeavours.

The king of the cats is dead, dead.
Old ladies leave scraps for the scattered
hundred in alleyways.
They are building the Royal Free where he
was tyrant.
Tom is dead. I am glad he is not alive
to see what they are doing.

Song Of The Women Of Islington

and I cry with passion
let there be wilderness
left for my children

across the sweet smelling
park, sways the shadow of the
mutant carp

and I cry with passion
let there be wilderness
left for my son

across the sweet waters of
Erie, falls the shadow of
humanity

and I cry with passion
let there be wilderness
left for my children

for across the child's
laughter, falls the roar of
the bulldozer

and I cry with passion
let there be sky and water
left for my daughter

across the secrets that children
know, falls the shadow of
the dodo

and I cry with passion
let there be wilderness
left for my children

There Are Some Creatures Living
In My Body

There are some creatures living in my body. I bid them
Welcome. Let them feed off me, as I off wild creatures
                                        that run free.
Let my veins and bones be to them rivers and baobabs let
cells be huge rich valleys, let gigantic landscapes
roll and change as I flex my nerves.
O I wish them an excellent universe, such a one
as I inhabit, mountains and wind and
a lot of stars. Nor let them
pollute and destroy what they find—let my rivers of blood
flow clean, my flesh be fertile and multiply, nor cloud
                                 with stale chemicals
the clear windows of my eyes.

The Return

The Return

Mother O here I come
in a bristle of eyes. Will the old wound
waken? Will the waterfall?
O here I come here I come mother
my nose streaming, eyelids bulging.
Will the old dog know me, will
the persimmon tree?
You wait in a shower of children.
Here I come out of the earth
out of the air—
here I come flaming
here I come bellowing
who will claim me?

The Reunion

Our family retainer has come bringing
marmalade. Lemon and grapefruit and stories
of our childhood.
With his long straight spine he bows, is
servant elect and honoured at the last wedding.
Gently he tells me
that vegetables rot in my grandmother's garden,
good green leaves and fruit, root and stem
where the earth opened for them.
Gently, that meanness like a disease
comes upon you from nowhere
an illness, without cause or cure or blame.
My grandmother hobbles into the kitchen
uninvited, hungry, greedy for leftovers
poking and prying. The hated one. In our country
servants prefer porridge.

The Shepherd

I saw an old man in a dock
his head bowed. One of his lambs
was bearing witness:

'I went to the dean for guidance
on personal and religious matters.
I went because I was a patriot.
I wrote down anything of interest
in my reports, first rough, then
neat—such things as
Communism, Revolution, Traitorous
Thoughts. My wife came with me to
church meetings. We joined the
congregation and took confirmation
classes. I wrote down anything of
interest.'

I saw an old man in a dock
a shepherd, lonely, lonely
calling the red-eyed wolf
to a grassland of sweet juices
and gentle water.

The Interrogation

> Who is screaming in the night
> Who is dying in the forest?

Lightning is the question
Sparks dance from your eyes
Terror is the price, pain
the prize.

> Who is screaming in the shadows
> Who is trembling in the darkness?

Words are the meat you eat
Words are your water
Time is forever
Death the comforter.

> Who is safe in his body
> Who is safe in the forest?

In the beautiful forest are wild flowers
Are birds eggs, sunlight
On the wind leaves are moving
Old the trees.

> Who is screaming in the forest
> Who is screaming in the forest?

from affidavits
written by fourteen prisoners
charged under the Terrorism Act,
South Africa, August 1971

Poor little bird, little penguin
little duck, small creature of water.
Poor small creature
alas thy dried wings, thy falling
feathers. Alas thy flaking
webbed feet.

Teach me of ripples and fish
Teach me the sound of lapping
Teach the seaweed tang, hang of the ocean
roar of water.
Teach me of air, of sailing
and gliding and wheeling.

Poor small creature
gathered
in pale dust, small creature of water.

The House Of Jealousy

This is the house of jealousy, these
her children.
Each has a basket of favours
and a cupboard of smiles.
Here is a collector of remembrances.
Here is the goodness gatherer.
Under the loquat tree is the sifter of thoughts
sitting sifting, grading
small thoughts from big ones
and here is the farmer sowing
good deeds in his ploughed pasture.
This is the house of jealousy, these
her children.

The Beast

In our house he stalks silent
on padded feet. He has left
cracks on the floorboards, gouged
chasms in my father's face, ripped
bloody rivers across his eyes.
My mother believes she has
tamed him. Nights, she strokes his coarse
fur, coaxes him onto her
bed, his huge weight
rocks on her chest. Purring like thunder
shakes the curtains. In pitiful mucousy
scratching her breathing
aggravates the night. There are
bloodspots on her pillow. Hers.
He's been king in our house
for thirty years now. I told them
—Don't keep pets, they will
devour you. Leave them
roam the wide bush. He heard.
He knocked me to the ground
with a massive paw
flexed his claws on my back
licked the blood with his bone-cold
reptile tongue. I cowered on the floor
screaming. His great jaws
smiled over me, yellow black-flecked
teeth had bits of
raw meat in them. His breath came in hot
foul smelling waves. Don't
show fear, said my mother, he
likes you.—He
lives here, said my father, he's

one of us. You'll have to
get to know him. I saw his arm was
scarred with claw marks
wrist to shoulder.
—He's old, said my father, be
gentle with him.
You'll learn.

The Trial

I am not afraid for my future.
I can tolerate my days and nights
but the sight of my spent years!
Prayers and whisperings lie heaped around me
so many soiled rags.
They have gone grovelling in filthy places
They have dug remnants of my body
from fever pits and graveyards
They have scraped me from the walls
of sewers, hacked my face from most
profane altars—my years—O prayers and bells
they have brought
like old bones in a sack
They have strewn them
a filthy heap
on the courtroom floor.
Never was priest so shamed by his flock
Never friend so humiliated.
I see my flowers in tatters
around me.
Let them paint me in blood
across the sky
let them torture me.
There is no honour here.
How I am dishonoured.
All my fresh children
with god blooming
in their eyes and on their dewy skin
were old and cracked and
laughing.
Laughing.

When I was a bum
When I was a drunk in the gutter
When I was the drunken sailor, the moon's
lewd adviser,
what a hymn raged in my throat!
Lord in thy service
a worm crawled up my anus
it gnawed at my belly
fattened on my defecation
now it is eating my liver
I grow sick, I spew Lord
It wriggles in my vomit
I am sick O Lord god
in thy service
the years! they are worm-ridden
the spent years!
I have lighted candles in thy service.
What a darkness is here, a hell-hole
gaping in my chest, what a silence.

Dean of the Anglican Church
charged under the Terrorism Act,
South Africa. August 1971

The Door

Somewhere in my head is a door.
Sealed. Invisible. Impossible
to prize and wrench
open. My head is a clean place.
I keep it tidy and neat. I need a
habitable environment for my
nice and neat little self.

Behind the door is another world.
Demons whirl there, gods rage and die and are
reborn. Flowers and gardens erupt
in frantic profusion. Processions of faces
loom out of darkness, hands grip my throat.

From the white peace of my head
I long for the door.
I am Alice, Pandora, I fling my fingers across
immaculate plaster—smooth emptiness.
The door has vanished—
never existed. I weep in my clean white
empty house.

Nights without warning the door will swing
open again letting forth to devour me
swarms of shrieking bats
in hideous glory.

Poem For Alice

You are all hunger—
little-cavernous-mouth little
shouter.
Love is your obsession
you burrow for it
the dark warm fluid
of your mother's body, little
nuzzler little
squirming-thing little
warbler.
You are her receptacle:
You are her circumference, her
container.
If the sky falls on her head
she will not give you up
she looks out at the world
across your need
little cavern-of-milk
little underground
river little
fighter.
You hold her taut between
light and the lonely
one like a kite string
little bearer-of-promises,
keeper of the treasure-house.

                for Libby Houston

We Found Him Amid Stones

We found him amid stones.
Covered in soft red dust
darting from ring to ring, arms
gesticulating
skin like winter grass
bones ungoverned.
There was no pretence in him
eyes clear blue, quick and curious
two birds.
Swiftly he moved.

The settlement was all circles
taught by the easy sun and the seasons
stone followed stone in
perfect symmetry.
Built to look out of
the sky a huge blue tent, sure curve
and swing of the mountains
its outer walls. Within, sleeping cells
granaries and mosaic ovens
curled in tight as wombs.

'Five hundred years these people
lived here without confusion
nor fought a war
nor sought a new world. Lived here
before the gathering of ships
hunting elephant, rearing cattle,
mining platinum in the echo-tone of
grassland and low bushveld,
stone-age and iron-age men with verandahs
sliding doors and precise, identical doorposts.

This little jar was for cosmetics;
here was a conical hut where the smith lived
and here, the tribal butcher who must have been
half bushman
carved up the elephant and deer
between these two stones.
At the summit here the chief lived
see how sheltered it is
and at this gate the cattle
were taken out to pasture.

They were here before the great trek
they were here through the long wars
they were here when the first seam of gold
ruptured like an artery across the land.
We have found bullets under ash . . .'
We found him amid stones.
With his small brush and careful trowel
he was sifting grains of truth
from a tangled jungle of red earth
time and prejudice and root and thorn.

                    for Revel Mason
                    Olifantskloof, August 1971

Ndumu

I went into the bush
to meet my black snake
he was where I knew he'd be
dead on time.

The sand was red and hot
the sun singing in my head
I recognized him
knew him deeply

then he struck.
The world burst like a melon.
He embraced me, lip to fang
then we parted.

Elephant Song

The yellow marula
makes the elephant drunk
ferments in his belly
gluttinous elephant
your coiling trunk
your mad eye
your bellowing joy
your sweating brow
your skull white now
under the marula tree.

Songs

Song Of The Drinker Of Juices

In the dark of the bark sweet
   sap in the dead of the scale
salty trickling
          drink my broth
in the cool of the moon
   light of the seed
oozing dank—unclot and bleed
milk of the fruit blood of the root
   juice of the bone
          boil and drain.

Under the onion's crackling skin
   needles of bitterness swim
in the stubborn turnip, shy
   flame of the carrot
   golden fluid
   are you weeping tomato?
I shall pop you out of your tense skin
   you are all water

ha little sphere, thought yourself
   a universe—I have discovered
imaginings of leaves and budding
   I shall burst you into a puddle
   squelch and you are flowing
   one now with the ox and the lamb
marrow bone, calf's brain
   boil, boil and drain

Lovely cow, factory of juices
   milk spurts from your breasts
and in your muscles blood bubbling
   I shall drain you dry as paper
   your bones will float in my saucepan
   I shall wrap your skin around me
to divide me in rain
   Quiet eyes, you are all water, water

See the green apple
   it is all water
see the cunning potato, hard as a stone
   it is all water
   see the thrice-blessed bird
   light as wind, wild as a god
it is all water, water
   I shall drink it

I am the drinker of juices
   I am the rot unclotting you
I'm the reducing factor
   brain of the ocean
   eyes of the rain
I am the drinker of juices
   thread unpicking your arteries
   alive and dead you're a ripple
   in my riverbed
   wave in my head
I drop by drop collecting of you
think and think of you
   eat no bread
love you and drink you.

Song Of The Almost Remembered

    Your trust betrayed me. Child
I am not your mother, nor ever
    could be. Never trust me

    don't come near me with your
dear crying. I am the one
    who dies when you need me

    I am the one who is not there
the absent one, that particular
    ache inside you, half knowledge

    of something lost that was never
quite answered. No I am not
    your mother, not your child

    never your beloved. I am the one
who passes across your dreams
    the almost remembered.

    Little smiling thing, arms
lifted like beating wings
    I am the far off

    light on the hills
in your private night where you are
    vomiting with fear.

    They will come back
with their strangeness and their healing
    and take you away and I will be

    utterly gone from you
again and again and again. There is no
    protection in me although

    little occupant
I am rigid with losing you
    everywhere we go.

Giving Song

I am the light of your night
I am the seed of your sight
I am your comfort and your direction
I am your dear one and your trusted

Here is my arm, your hands are clumsy
here are my five fingers, see
I will chop them off and give them
your hands will be little birds

Here are my feet
well trained and nimble
they know all the roads and the hazards
they will take you wherever you have to go

Here is my heart
you are sluggish in loving
this will make you feel and tremble
you will be as Christ to your beloved

Here is my head, complete
with thoughts well constructed everything
perfectly worked out all in order
it will last a lifetime

with its fine articulate mouth and
discriminating eyes.
What else will you need—laughter
I can give you plenty of, I know

where it is kept, and courage
is a key—here take it, I won't be needing
much now. For the rest, health I have already
packed up in your basket

and when you come to the river
call me. I shall come again and carry you
across. Are you alright now? Are you happy?
Dear don't cry, don't leave me.

Song Of The Flying Baboon

I am the flying baboon
Hyee I kill, I kill people
hold my brown wrinkled fingers
over their nostrils
cover their mouths with a palm
reeking of bark

I soar through the high air
hyee without effort
I remember swimming
in my mother's body
Everything is dim but the air
is solid, solid.

I know they want to get me.
They are amassing on the ground
like a nest of fire-engines
at the airport
I am swimming as hard as I can now
breast-stroking it over the rooftops

and the trees like black beacons
of my sinking.
I am swiftly losing altitude
I am almost upon them
I try cunning, hiding in the shadows
but the down-pull of my body is so heavy

hyee so heavy I fight I fight
and now I am upon them
they grab me with their million hands
and million hard eyes
I sense a net closing irrevocably.
I am the captured

heavy baboon limp as a pudding
without resistance
no more glad killings no more flying in air
to be fallen gross and defeated
is my sin. Irredeemable. Punish.
See how the sky has receded to a dark ocean.

Hymn For A Stranger

I picked you out from the human
avalanche at leicester square. I followed you.

You were dressed in flared jeans patched with
butterflies and lace flowers. Your waistcoat was

hand crocheted in many colours your boots painted
bright red. I measured your thighs not to be

too long, your wrists to be slender your feet
lightly lifted and carefully placed down. Then I moved

slowly across your face. Your smile
delighted me, curling at the corners and never

held in. With a little help from me, good luck
sat you down beside me on the train.

After that it was a chain of little
decisions and courageous eye-flashes until you

got off at my station and we were left
confronting each other. Tea and pot and soft music and

the honesty game helped, and the beeswax candles and
rich strange sweetness in a little glass.

I touched your finger suddenly, needing to tell you
that I had decided, and you startled me with

that blinding smile and suddenly wide open eyes.
Making love on the white carpet at dawn was

everything that I wanted, uncomplicated with tangled
emotions like roots eating into me, and the

tearing. You were beautiful and sure and skilled
I thrived in your arms like a tree and you

blossomed inside me. I thrived and sang and the sun
opened over the rooftops like a wound and you

went home in a taxi, waving. Stranger on the platform
you have filled me with glowing

and now you linger in my rooms and in my body rejoicing
like smoke on a sun shaft.

Complaint Of The Water

   I am confounded by drains
everywhere opening under my fins
   netting my progress

   labyrinths of stinking darkness:
I am confounded by the rush of myself
   everywhere the down-pull

   hurl of me and sinking
my gross weight and hopeless
   onrush of longing to

   lose myself in the sea.
All that I love I flee from: air
   that opens its wings, mountains

   and rock, and all that is steadfast
I knot myself against, fling myself
   out and away from. All things

   eat me: veins and capillaries
suck me from my chosen
   adventures and fasten me into

   usurping fat flowers and leaves.
O you false blossoming dryness
   that I must creep through unseen

   and humbly, one day I shall
drown the world—all things will live
   and swim in me.

Song Of The Taken Care Of

All the trees are gone
but they have built the royal free
they are taking care of me
taking care of me

all the beautiful stray cats have gone
and the dear old ladies who used to feed them
they have gone to the vivisection ward
and the old are on royal free pension

everything is being taken care of
everyone will be alright
don't worry about the places you used to love
or the owls you used to hear in the trees at night

you are being taken care of
everything is being taken care of you see
and remember the moment you feel unhappy
they'll find you a bed in her majesty's royal free

they are taking care of me
although I don't know who they are
they are taking care of me for good
taking good care of me.

In South Africa
when it rains and
the sun shines at the
same time, they call it
Monkeys' Wedding.
In Ghana they say
Ogboole is doing
her washing.

Children run outside
shouting
'Monkeys' Wedding!'
to play in the
bright rain.